On the Day You Were Born

Debra Frasier

Harcourt Brace & Company

San Diego   New York   London

With special thanks to Allyn Johnston,
for her steadfast editing and
long-distance bird-watching   — D. F.

Requests for permission to make copies of any part
of the work should be mailed to: Permissions Department,
Harcourt Brace & Company, 6277 Sea Harbor Drive,
Orlando, Florida 32887-6777.

Library of Congress Cataloging-in-Publication Data
Frasier, Debra.
On the day you were born/by Debra Frasier. — 1st ed.
p.   cm.
Summary: The earth celebrates the birth of a newborn baby.
ISBN 0-15-257995-8
1. Earth — Juvenile literature. 2. Birth — Juvenile literature.
[1. Earth. 2. Birth.] I. Title.
QB631.4.F74   1991
508 — dc20   90-36816
Q

Printed in Singapore

On an island off Wabasso, in Florida's Indian River Lagoon, concerned citizens have built
the Environmental Learning Center, a place where children and adults can see and learn
about the aquatic life thriving in this part of Florida. A portion of the proceeds from the sale
of this book will support the Center's Conservation through Education programming fund.

For Mother Earth,
born 4½ billion years ago

and Baby Calla,
born June 1, 1988

and You

On the eve of your birth
word of your coming
passed from animal to animal.

The reindeer told the Arctic terns,
who told the humpback whales,
who told the Pacific salmon,

who told the monarch butterflies,
who told the green turtles,
who told the European eel,
who told the busy garden warblers,

and the marvelous news migrated worldwide.

While you waited in darkness,
tiny knees curled to chin,
the Earth and her creatures
with the Sun and the Moon
all moved in their places,
each ready to greet you
the very first moment
of the very first day you arrived.

On the day you were born
the round planet Earth
turned toward your morning sky,
whirling past darkness,
spinning the night into light.

On the day you were born
gravity's strong pull
held you to the Earth
with a promise that you
would never float away...

. . . while deep in space
the burning Sun
sent up
towering flames,
lighting your sky
from dawn until dusk.

On the day you were born
the quiet Moon glowed
and offered to bring
a full, bright face,
each month,
to your windowsill...

. . . while high above the North Pole,
Polaris, the glittering North Star,
stood still, shining silver light
into your night sky.

On the day
you were born
the Moon pulled
on the ocean
below, and,
wave by wave,
a rising tide
washed the
beaches clean for
your footprints...

. . . while far
out at sea
clouds swelled
with water drops,
sailed to shore
on a wind,
and rained you
a welcome
across the Earth's
green lands.

On the day you were born
a forest of tall trees
collected the Sun's light
in their leaves,
where, in silent mystery,
they made oxygen
for you to breathe...

. . . while close to your skin
and as high as the sky,
air rushed in and blew about,
invisibly protecting you
and all living things on Earth.

On the day you were born
the Earth turned, the Moon pulled,
the Sun flared, and, then, with a push,

you slipped out of the dark quiet
where suddenly you could hear . . .

...a circle of people singing
with voices familiar and clear.

"Welcome to the spinning world," the people sang,
as they washed your new, tiny hands.

"Welcome to the green Earth," the people sang,
as they wrapped your wet, slippery body.

And as they held you close
they whispered into your open, curving ear,
"We are so glad you've come!"

More about the World around You

MIGRATING ANIMALS

An animal's **migration pattern** has two parts: an outward journey and a return journey. The most common reasons animals migrate are to find food and to breed, but there are still many unanswered questions as to *why* some animals make such spectacular trips and *how* they know to return to the very place where they started.

Reindeer of Lapland, Finland, travel north in the spring to eat Arctic moss, returning at the end of the Arctic summer. *Arctic terns* fly and ride the winds 17,000 miles, traveling from their Arctic breeding sites north of England and Scandinavia to their Antarctic winter feeding sites off the tip of South America and then back again. *Humpback whales* feed in the icy waters of the most northern and southern oceans and swim toward the equator during their respective winters to birth and nurse their young in warmer waters. *Pacific salmon* hatch in freshwater inland streams of the United States's northwest and travel all the way to the Pacific Ocean to live. After two years these salmon probably use the stars and special odors to find the stream where they hatched and return to produce their own young. Each fall, one hundred million *monarch butterflies* from the eastern and central United States fly southward across the continent to their winter roosts in the fir forests of central Mexico. The spectacular journey of the *green turtles* takes these giant ocean swimmers from their feeding grounds off the shores of Brazil to a beach 870 miles away, on tiny Ascension Island, where they lay their eggs. After twenty to perhaps thirty years, turtles hatched there will swim back to the very same beach to lay their own eggs, somehow finding this tiny stretch of sand in the enormous Atlantic Ocean. *European eels* hatch off the coast of Florida, and when they are four inches long, they set off on a transatlantic journey that can take up to three years. The eels search for a European freshwater stream where they will live until they grow to adult size, and then make the long return trip to North America. *European garden warblers* begin their journey in central Africa and fly all the way across the Sahara and the Mediterranean Sea, returning in a giant circle by way of the Strait of Gibraltar and across the desert again.

SPINNING EARTH

The earth rotates west to east on its **axis**, an imaginary line that runs through the earth from the North Pole to the South Pole. Exactly halfway down the axis, between the poles, there is another imaginary line that makes a circle, like a belt, around the earth. This line is called the **equator**. The earth rotates very fast—approximately 1,040 miles per hour at the equator—without ever stopping or slowing down. When any point on earth faces the sun, it is day, and when that same point turns away from the sun, the sun appears to set, and night begins. The earth takes 24 hours to make one complete turn. While the earth is turning daily, it is also traveling in a yearly orbit around the sun.

PULLING GRAVITY

Every object in the universe is pulled to every other object. This force of attraction is called **gravity**. Even though all objects attract each other, people are most affected by the pull from the closest, most massive object, which is the earth. The earth, in turn, is most affected by the gravitational pull from the sun and moon. On earth, all bodies have **weight**, which is actually the downward force of gravity pulling an object toward the earth's core, or center. Because of this constant pull toward the core, no matter where you stand on earth, when you point overhead, it's up! The earth's gravity has a long reach, even pulling the moon, 238,857 miles away, toward the earth's center.

No one has actually seen inside our planet, but scientists have outlined a model of its interior through experiments that measure the speed of vibrations passing through the earth. According to this model, there are four distinct layers, beginning with the rock **crust**, directly under the surface soil and water. The **mantle**, a hot, heavy, flexible layer, rests under the crust. The center is in two parts — an **outer core** of molten iron, and, finally, a red-hot iron ball called the **inner core**.

FLAMING SUN

The sun, the closest star to earth, measures 400 times the width of our planet. Its surface is a huge mass of burning gases that are stacked up like the cloud layers surrounding the earth. The fiery outside layers of gas race around, swirling at 4,000 miles per hour, sending up huge flames. These giant jets of fire are called **prominences** and arch a million miles above the surface. Light from the burning sun takes about 8 minutes to travel the 93-million-mile distance to the earth's surface. All life on earth depends on the energy of sunlight.

GLOWING MOON

The moon travels in a circle around the earth. It will not drift off into space because of the constant pull of the earth's gravity. The moon also rotates slowly, turning on its own axis at the same rate it travels around the earth, showing the same side toward earth at all times. It does not make its own light but, instead, catches light from the sun and reflects it back to earth, like a mirror. The sun is constantly shining light on the moon, making one side bright while the other side is always dark.

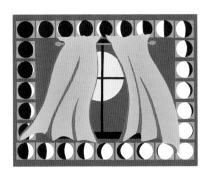

When the earth is between the sun and the moon, a fully lit moon shines toward earth. When the moon travels around between the sun and earth, no light is reflected toward earth. This dark moon is called a **new moon**. As the moon travels between full and new and back again it reflects a varying amount of light toward earth each night. These nightly changes in the moon's appearance are called **phases**. The moon's complete trip around the earth takes about 28 days.

GLITTERING STAR

People have often separated stars into groups that outline pictures in the night sky. These star groups are called **constellations**. Ursa Minor, which contains the Little Dipper, is one such constellation. It looks like a drinking cup with a long handle. The star **Polaris** is located in the northern sky at the end of the Little Dipper's handle. If the earth's axis, that imaginary line running between the North Pole and the South Pole, were extended far into deep space above the North Pole, it would point almost directly to Polaris. While the earth spins on this axis, Polaris seems perched on the end of it, not moving. When a person looks at the night sky from anywhere north of the equator, all the other stars seem to move in a giant circle around this **North Star** or **Pole Star**. Polaris's place in the sky is very dependable and can be used as a fixed point to measure distances in the northern hemisphere.

RISING TIDE

The earth is pulled slightly toward the moon by the moon's gravity. The oceans are more responsive to this tug than the land, and are constantly rising and falling in response to the moon's position above them.

When the moon is directly above an ocean, the moon's gravity attracts the water, pulling the ocean slightly away from the earth. This tugging makes a deeper ocean and a **high tide** at the shoreline directly beneath the moon. At the same time, there is a high tide on the *opposite* side of the earth. There, the pull of the moon's gravity on the ocean is weaker, and the water bulges out as the force of the earth's spin pushes the water outward. This is why, if you were to stay on the beach all day and night, there would usually be two high tides: one when the moon is directly overhead and one a little more than 12 hours later, when your beach has rotated directly opposite the moon and is farthest from the effect of the moon's gravity. Each day there are **low tides** when the planet is rotating between these two high-water marks. It takes 24 hours and 50 minutes for any given beach on earth to rotate through these tides and have the moon directly overhead again.

FALLING RAIN

Water can exist in three different states. It can be solid, like ice; liquid, like water to drink; or invisible, as a gas called **water vapor**. Water can be found in all these forms in the sky. When water in the ocean is heated by the sun, the smallest units of water (called **molecules**) lift up, or **evaporate**, right into the air. This invisible water vapor cools, attaches itself to bits of dust, sea salt, or smoke, and becomes a **droplet**. The cooling and turning of water vapor into tiny droplets is called **condensation**. When these droplets travel in large groups in the sky, we see them as clouds. Scientists are still studying how a drop falls, but many think that the tiny droplets begin to stick together until the newly formed drop becomes so heavy it falls to earth as *precipitation*. Often the tops of clouds are made of ice crystals, and another theory suggests that when these ice crystals grow too heavy, they fall earthward. When a falling drop or ice crystal passes through cold air on the way down, it reaches earth as snow or sleet. When a falling drop or ice crystal passes through warm air, it reaches earth as rain. Every day it rains somewhere on earth.

GROWING TREES

Trees usually have a single trunk, rooted in the ground, that supports a crown of smaller branches. From these branches grow leaves, and they grow in many, many different shapes and sizes depending on the type of tree. Leaves in northern climates are often flat and broad in order to capture as much sunlight as possible. Leaves in dry areas are often small and thin in order to limit sun exposure and loss of moisture. Regardless of size, each leaf catches sunlight and draws in the gas carbon dioxide from the air while water and minerals travel up from the tree's roots. The combination of sunlight, carbon dioxide, water, and minerals goes through a chemical change inside the leaves and produces sugar as food for the tree. The leaves make and release the gas oxygen in the process. This process is called *photosynthesis*.

Every day trees are absorbing a great deal of carbon dioxide and releasing oxygen. When people breathe, they *inhale*, or take in, the gas oxygen and *exhale*, or give out, carbon dioxide so people and trees are constantly exchanging air. Each acre of young forest makes about four tons of oxygen per year. This is enough oxygen for 18 people to breathe for one year, so there must be many, many acres of trees to contribute to the oxygen needs of all the people and animals on planet earth.

RUSHING AIR

About 600 million years ago, enough oxygen mixed with other gases to form the thick layer of air, or *atmosphere*, that surrounds our planet today. Oxygen, the gas human beings need to breathe, makes up about 21 percent of the atmosphere. Nitrogen, another gas, makes up most of the rest. This layer of gases is very important. It acts like a blanket, sheltering the earth from too much heat from the sun and holding in warmth so the planet's temperature does not drop too low at night. The atmosphere gets thinner farther from the earth. The closest layer of air, called the *troposphere*, extends to between 5 and 11 miles outward and contains most of the earth's weather. The next layer is the *stratosphere*, followed by the *ionosphere*, and, finally, the *exosphere*, extending 5,500 miles from earth. Beyond the exosphere is *space* where there is no air.

SINGING PEOPLE

Each day babies are born in every country on earth. The number of people, or the **population**, on our planet is increasing each year, yet each person is unique.

One of the most noticeable differences among people is the color of their skin. This color comes from tiny grains of **melanin**, a pigment found in the second and third layer of a person's skin. These grains are so small that, to the eye, they blend together and make the skin look smoothly colored. Many scientists think that the different shades of human skin evolved as a response to the sun's intensity.

Thousands and thousands of years ago, when only small tribes of people lived scattered across the tropical areas of the earth, the color of a person's skin could offer important protection from the powerful ultraviolet rays of the sun. To these early equatorial people, darker skin proved to be a shield from this danger. Survival depended on just such advantages, and dark-skinned people flourished. As people moved toward the poles, where winters are long and sunlight scarce, lighter-skinned people benefited from their ability to more easily absorb the sunlight necessary for a healthy body. More of these pale-skinned people survived the demands of winter, and successive generations in colder climates favored fairer-skinned people. Thus people's skin evolved to range from very deep brown, or nearly black, to light brown, shades of beige, or even light pink, depending on where they lived on the planet. Scientists expect skin color to slowly continue to adapt to the changing conditions on earth.

The paper collages in this book were made with Crescent and Canson papers.
The text and display type were set in Goudy Old Style by Thompson Type, San Diego, California.
Color separations were made by Bright Arts, Ltd., Singapore.
Printed and bound by Tien Wah Press, Singapore
Production supervision by Warren Wallerstein and Ginger Boyer
Designed by Debra Frasier and Joy Chu